A BOY'S LIFE DURING WWII

A Survival Story

EDUARD SCHRAMA

ISBN: 978-1-09831-045-5 (print)
ISBN: 978-1-09831-046-2 (eBook)

CONTENTS

BEGINNING

I was born in Holland, four years before World War II would start, into a family of four brothers, a sister, and both parents. It was March 1936. My mother was forty-six years old and much too old to have a baby. My youngest brother Bob was five years old, sister Nettie ten, brothers Fred were seventeen, Wil eighteen and Nico nineteen. The family expected me to be damaged. Instead, I was healthy and very active.

My dad was fifty years old and sick when I arrived. He slept in our small living room on a couch. A restless baby in this crowded place was a bad mix. When I started crawling, and then walking, my bumping into Dad's bed became a big problem. When his swearing became too much for Mother, she locked me in our unheated front room to keep me away from him. I was two years old. To her surprise, I did not complain. I sat on a chair, looking through the front window at street activity. On the opposite corner of the street was a store that sold hot water. Every morning women lined up with buckets. They talked very loudly, and I could easily hear them through the thin glass, but I could not understand them.

Our living room had a coal heater, but the rest of the house was unheated. Mother bundled me up in the morning, and I was happy in my "cell." Until I was three years old, the family paid little attention to me. My three oldest brothers worked. On weekends they biked to town, returning with their bikes' side bags loaded with food, which was stored in our attic. They did this for a full year until the stores ran out of supplies.

Brother Bob was now eight and Nettie thirteen years old. It bothered Nettie that I looked at the street all day, and she taught me numbers and simple reading. Brother Bob didn't like me and constantly told me I was stupid to sit on my chair looking at the street. On my fourth birthday I got two presents: a bike, and I was allowed to walk alone anywhere I wanted.

Brother Wil got water for doing the laundry, and he took me a few times to the water store. There I met Jan, the man who sold the hot water. I liked him. I sat on a bench and he told me how the boilers worked. My bike didn't have training wheels, and for the first few weeks I crashed many times. I hid my cuts and scrapes from Mother. She put iodine on cuts, and I had to swallow cod liver oil if I didn't feel well from anything else. I didn't tell her about my cuts. I'd rather hurt.

My biking improved, and I zoomed constantly around our block. Wil told me I had to bike on our block's sidewalk until I was five years old. I had learned from early on that one warning was all you got, so I stuck to the rules.

I had been biking for two months, and each day was the same. Sometimes there was a horse-drawn cart and a few bikers or some people walking by. Nobody paid attention to me, which I liked. This late morning started out as usual. It was nice weather, and I was looking forward to a quiet afternoon. When I came around the corner, our street had suddenly filled with a lot of people, and I had to walk home. My whole family was standing outside, even my sick father. My brothers had come home from work. I asked Wil what was going on. "None of your business, go inside," he said. When I didn't move, Mother asked if I would like dinner. That was enough for me, and I went inside. I was always hungry.

When they came in the house they were quiet, and at dinner-time nobody talked. That was strange. Every night, Father and my brothers always had loud talks about Germany, invasion and war, and the starvation in the country that Father expected. I paid little attention to all this until I started to hear the same words from the women who stood in line for water. I could hear them right through our thin front room window glass. I asked sister Nettie what was going on, but she didn't know either. "It's very bad, but I don't know why. It makes me nervous that they won't tell us," she said.

I decided to ask Jan in the water store. "It's terrible for Holland. The Germans just walked into our country. We have no army to speak of and we live next to Germany. There was nothing to stop them. They bombed the city of Rotterdam and killed thousands. Our government should have seen this coming a long time ago, but they're idiots." He was very upset and went behind the boilers, and I went biking. The whole thing felt strange to me. The street was the same as always. Quiet.

I met a kid who lived on our street. He had red hair and his nickname was "Red." He became my best friend. Other kids from the area showed up sometimes, but I saw Red every day. He teased me for a while about not leaving the sidewalk when I biked. "You're a wimp. I won't tell anyone," he said. "Yeh," I said, "you only have to worry about your mother. She lets you do anything you want. I'm not a wimp to stay on the sidewalk. If my brother finds out that I didn't, I'll get no dinner." He stopped bothering me.

The weather was getting colder and Red quit biking. I teased him that he was now the wimp, and he called me crazy. We laughed about it and I biked alone. A kid from the neighborhood showed up and we biked around the block a few times. Then he began to bother me with crowding me on narrow parts of the sidewalk. I almost crashed. The next day he tried to do it again, but I was ready for him. When he passed me, I turned my wheel into his and he crashed. His front wheel was warped, and he yelled, "I'll beat the hell out of you!" When I got ready for him, he took his bike and walked away. I had play-wrestled with Red a few times, and he had trouble keeping me down. I was skinny but strong and not afraid of the kid.

Some days I heard loud noises coming from the main road that was nearby. After hearing it a few times, my nosiness was stronger than my fear. I walked to the corner of the main road and saw trucks full of soldiers driving by. Some of them waved as they passed me. I couldn't understand it. They seemed friendly. The next time I went, the same thing happened. They waved to me. I was very confused.

With Nettie's help I learned to count, and I began counting the trucks when they passed by. It was fun for me. Sometimes there were more than fifty, which I couldn't do. When I told Jan, he got very interested. "You know how many trucks passed you?" he asked. "Yes, but when there are too many I can't do it," I told him. "Well, next time come right here to tell me what you saw," Jan said. From then on I counted the trucks and told Jan what I saw. I liked to make him happy. "Don't tell anybody about this," he told me. "I will be our secret."

When I stood on the corner, I could see a park across the main road. A fence gate was locked, but there were large holes in the fence. I could see a large grass field behind the fence. One day, when only a few trucks came by, I went across the main road and crawled through the fence. Standing on the grass, I heard the noises coming from behind the far side of the field.

They were different noises than the trucks made, and I had to find out what made them. I found a rail yard with a locomotive moving railcars around. The engineer on the train waved to me. Behind the tracks of the rail yard was a high dike, and high-speed trains passed by every few minutes while I was looking at the locomotive moving the cars around. I told Red what I'd seen, but he wouldn't go to the yard with me. "I'm sure we'll get into trouble," he said.

FIVE

My birthday present was allowing me to bike everywhere. No more being stuck on our block's sidewalk. I biked mostly alone since Red had school. In a few months I would have to start school too. Wil had shown me the building. It looked scary to me—a dark building with a few windows. Listening to Bob's pestering would be better than being locked up for hours in that place.

I biked all over town, way outside to where the farms were. The Germans parked most of their trucks on farmland, and each day I gave my numbers to Jan. Summer went by fast without any big changes. I had asked Red a few times to go to the rail yard to see what was in the train cars, but he didn't want to do it. Finally he agreed. We went on a Saturday when there was little traffic on the road to the factory behind the dike. There were many railcars in the yard, and we checked a few. They were all loaded with heavy machinery. Nothing good to steal. I told Wil where we had been, but he wasn't interested.

In the fall I had to go to school. In the beginning I didn't mind it too much, but that changed quickly. I was left-handed, and the teacher made me write with my right hand. When I switched to my left hand he threw a straight edge at me, hitting me in the arm. When I returned it, he rapped my hand with the straight edge and said, "Next time you don't listen to me, you'll remember how this felt." After that I hated the place.

In the fall of 1941, Father stopped eating meals with us. Mother made food for him that was easy to swallow. Drinking was also hard for him. He slept most of the time. When he talked to Mother, she had to put her ear close to his mouth. He could only whisper a few words, and that also stopped. I had never seen anybody dying, but it did not bother me. To me, it was almost as if a stranger was lying on the couch. Everybody seemed to be waiting for him to die. I could see that.

He died in February 1942. It happened on a day when I was out biking. When I walked into the living room, brother Fred was lying on the sofa bed. Father was gone. I was confused. I asked Mother if Dad had been brought to the hospital. "No," she said. "He died today, and you should be glad." That was it. I knew this would happen, but it still came as a shock. It bothered me that he was suddenly gone. No tears from anybody. *Maybe if I got run over by a truck, nobody would care either*, I thought.

We had used up most of the food supplies that were stored in the attic. We now were getting small amounts of food from soup kitchens that had opened in our area. It was thin and watery—small amounts and not enough for the family.

During the winter of 1942, the Germans were stealing every-thing from our country. Fuel for heaters was impossible to get. People started burning furniture, tires, and trees. They also broke up roads that were paved with wooden blocks, soaked in an oil that prevented rotting. When these were burned, the smoke was thick and covered big areas of the town. Nobody cared. Better than freezing.

The winter months of 1943 were brutally cold. My seventh birthday came and went. Hunger was everywhere in the country. Even though it was very dangerous for my three oldest brothers to bike to farms, they did make a few trips, waiting for a snow-free night. The farmers were only willing to sell sugar beets, which they had always grown as animal food. They were the size of a small squash. They had never been used by people, but now we were hungry enough to eat almost anything. With few other vegetables available, they were mixed with onions and carrots. Mother cut the beets into thin strips and made a stew with it. It became the dinner for many days. I hated it. It tasted horribly sweet. I couldn't stand the taste, but it took care of the hunger pains.

THE SWEATERS

It was December 1943. The weather had been snowy and cold. I woke at eight o'clock, Saturday morning. I saw the window had the usual layer of ice on the inside. I quickly got dressed, scratching my name in the ice. It knew it would still be there in the evening when I went to bed.

When I got downstairs, Mother and Wil were talking at the table. I never listened to Mother's talks with Wil, but when I heard my name mentioned a few times, I started to pay attention. It had to do with getting food for the family. The farmers were talked about. After a while, Wil called me over to the table and explained what was decided. He found a way for us to trade with the farmers, he said. "The success of our plan will depend on you, my boy."

He asked, "Tell me, how many times have you been in the rail yard?"

"Red and I have been around the railcars during the day on weekends, when they weren't moving them." Wil looked at me and said, "Good, I have to know how many railcars are on the tracks, and how far they are parked from the road." I couldn't figure out what he wanted from me, especially since he had been talking to Mother. When Wil told me his plan, and what I had to do, it scared me half to death. "We've decided that the only way we can try to trade with the farmers is if Mother knits sweaters, but we need yarn to make them," Wil said. "I know where to get the yarn, but nobody, except

8

you, can get it for her." Hearing that I was the only one really got me very angry. I yelled at him, "Why can't Bob do it?"

"Simple," Wil said. "You've been in the yard. You know how to get in without being seen by anybody." I knew that was not the only reason. Mother made sure that Bob wouldn't be sent on such a crazy trip. Wil started telling me how I could get the yarn. "The wheel bearings of the rail cars are filled with thick oil. Yarn keeps the oil from sloshing around. The yarn is packed tightly around the axle in the brake box. If you get that yarn for us, Mother can knit sweaters with it, and with those we can try to trade with the farmers. You'll need to take your sled and buckets and have to go when its dark." Going alone into the rail yard in the pitch-black late evening scared me so much that I started crying. Wil got me water and when I calmed down, I told him that I had never been in the yard when it was dark. "It's filled with pieces of rail and junk. I can't see those in the dark. I know I will fall and get hurt." No matter what I said, he wouldn't listen. "I feel terrible for making you do this, but it's the only chance we have to get food," he said.

It was the first time that I hated him. I couldn't believe they would send me out in the dark, at seven years old, to a place I had only been a few times. I saw bad pictures in my mind, being caught by Germans with dogs. I wouldn't know how to explain what I was doing there. "I don't want to do it," I said to Wil. "What if they catch me?"

"I don't think they have patrols in the dark," Wil said. And that was that. No matter what I said, he didn't listen.

That night I had horrible nightmares. I thought he would bring it up again the next morning, but nothing was said. *Maybe they agreed it's too dangerous?* I thought. Two weeks went by. I started to relax, hoping I wouldn't have to go. No such luck. After a nice bike ride, Wil decided to shake me up again. "Mother didn't want you to go to the yard and I had a long talk with her about it. She finally said yes, knowing we have no choice." He had a picture of a railcar that clearly showed the covers on the wheel boxes. "Can you see the handle on the cover?" he asked. I saw a cover with a big spring on the top, holding it closed. "I will make a tool for you to pry the cover off. You'll need all your strength since the spring is very strong." Hearing that didn't make me feel very good. "You also need a tool to pull the yarn out. The oil is thick in the cold weather. It will be hard to get out. You can only get a little out at a time since it's packed tight around the axle."

"What do I do if I can't open the cover?"

"You pull harder," Wil said. That was all he could tell me. When he finished explaining, it hit me what it meant. They were sending me in the darkness into a dark rail yard. I had trouble believing it. It made me shiver. Wil took me into the hallway and said, "Would you want to have Bob in the yard with you?" He knew my answer; it was NO. I told him so. "Good. Let's go to the attic. I'll make the tools you need and explain how to get the yarn out of the compartments." With our vise, he bent a couple of screwdrivers, changing the ends to hooks. He sharpened them with a small hand-powered grinder. I always liked to crank the grinder when he used it. It was always fun. Not this time. The trip was on my mind.

Wil said that if I ran ever into a patrol, I should cry (which I was good at) and tell them that I was lost and scared. "Saturday will be the perfect time for your first trip to the rail yard," Wil said. The scary part for me was not that I would be alone. What I feared was being stopped by a patrol and not be able to explain what I was doing in the late evening with my sled and tools in a rail yard.

Late Saturday I left the house at nine o'clock with my tools and one bucket tied onto the sled. Wil told me to wear a ski mask to protect my face from the cold and biting wind. The trip had been on my mind all day. I had made myself extremely nervous by imagining bad things that could happen, and it made me angry that Mother refused to even talk about having Bob do the job with me.

FIRST TRIP

The park across the main road was completely fenced in on all four sides. One side I knew well. A few times I got into the park through a hole in the fence. That's how I planned to get to the yard, with my tools and sled. Once in the park, I could easily reach the far side that was along the rail tracks and nobody could see me from the road. Wil walked me the short distance to the main road, even though it was very dangerous for him to be outside. "I can't go further, I'm sorry," he said and turned around. When I got across the main road I realized that the sled wouldn't fit through the fence hole. The only way to the rail yard was the road into the yard. Bad setback. This night the weather was bad, which I liked. It would make the trip harder, but I wouldn't have to worry about many people on the roads.

It had never bothered me to be alone. Mostly, I liked to be alone, but now on the dark road, I was scared. The red bricks on the road were covered with snow, and an open farm field on the side of the road didn't block the howling wind. The park side of the road had large snow piles against the fence. With that much snow, I had no chance of using the sidewalk. The farm field was used by the Germans to store their trucks and materials. It was also used by their security people who patrolled the rail yard and the nearby factories. They stayed in trailers, which I knew were on the far side of the field. I had been worried that they could see me, but there were no lights and I couldn't see any trailers; it was so dark. My big worry was getting caught. If I saw a car coming up the road, I would leave the sled on the side of the road and lay flat in the snow, against the park fence, hoping they wouldn't see me.

The sled was getting stuck in the snow, and my arms got tired from pulling and lifting it over the snow heaps that had piled up on the road. I was only halfway toward the entrance to the yard and almost ready to give up. The wind was much stronger than when I crossed the main road. The noises from the trees made me imagine scary animals were after me. Nettie had read a book to me about a kid who was lost in the woods, with wolves all around him. It felt to me like they were in the park, ready to jump over the fence. I was terribly afraid. The only thing that kept me going was knowing that without me doing this, we would starve. Wil had told me that enough times.

The struggle up the road took much longer than I had planned. I started to think that the end would never be there. Finally, I saw the opening between the high steel fence and the park's fence. I was at the tracks. It had taken much longer than I thought, and I hadn't even reached the first railcar yet. The few times I'd been in the yard, the weather had been fine. Dry and sunny. Even then, walking on the wooded ties between the rails had been hard. They were uneven, with large rocks between them. Now, with snow covering them, it was very difficult. The rails were hard to see, but following them was safer than falling on the sharp rocks. I slid my feet against both sides of the rail, working my way to the first railcar. I fell a few times. My elbow was hurting badly. I could see the first car in the distance when the snow wasn't circling. Just a shadow, but I knew I was close. I even had a crazy thought that there wouldn't be any railcars on the tracks and then I wouldn't have to do this anymore. Finally, I got to the first car. Snow was deep on the side where I would have to pry open the bearing box. I picked this side because the car blocked the wind. It started to snow harder and it was piling up fast. I got the crowbar out of the bucket, pulling with all my might on the cover. It wouldn't budge. *Maybe the springs were just too strong for me to break the rubber seal,* I thought. Wil had told me that it could happen. I was close to giving up but decided to try the next car. This car's set of wheels were not buried in heaps of snow. The swirling snow dumped it in some places, leaving others bare. Maybe I would get lucky. The cover on this brake box moved a little when I pulled. I put the pipe over the crowbar and yanked as hard as I could. It opened far enough to stick a screwdriver in the crack. I was very tired, half-frozen, and wearing Mother's knitted gloves. They were soaked from the melting snow. My fingertips were frozen. I had to warm my hands before I could do anything else. Everything was taking much longer than I expected. *I don't even know yet if I can get the yarn out,* I was thinking. After a while I could feel my fingertips again and tried to open the cover. I got it open far enough to get my fingers in the opening. I felt a sticky paste. It didn't feel like oil. Wil was right. It would be hard to get the yarn out with that paste being stuck around the axle. With my hooked screwdriver I was able to get behind a clump of yarn. By twisting it, I pulled some yarn out. They were short pieces, not much longer than my hand. *How can Mother knit with that,* I thought. *Maybe she can't use it and I don't have to go anymore.* I pulled about two handfuls out of the compartment and stopped. Wil had warned me not to take all the yarn out of the compartments. "Bearings can be damaged when the oil sloshes around. The Germans will find out quickly what happened when they check them," he had told me. I managed to close the cover with my crowbar and went to the next car. Both covers on this car opened easier. I started to feel a little better. *Maybe I can get enough for Mother to try it out,* I hoped. I opened the covers on four cars, filling my bucket almost to the top with the oil-soaked yarn. The bucket was heavy and smelly. My gloves were soaked with the oil. Surprisingly, the oil seemed to warm up my hands a little. *I must ask Wil how that's possible.*

Going back was harder than I expected. The snow was now deeper. The rails were completely covered. I had hoped to go back the way I came, but my tracks were covered with snow. I moved over two tracks and got close to the high metal fence. I thought that would block the wind and dump less snow. Not so. Also, what I had forgotten was that the spare rails and clamps were scattered everywhere on this side. Stepping on them caused me to fall a few times. My bucket fell over twice. Picking up the snow-soaked wool refroze my fingers again. Reaching the road was terribly hard. I was close to sitting down in the snow to rest, but Wil had warned me about that. "Whatever you do, never take a rest in freezing weather. You'll fall asleep and die," he warned me. That kept me moving, finally reaching the road.

I thought the trip to the main road would be quicker and not as hard, but it was even more difficult. Pulling the heavy bucket through the snow on the road was wearing me out. I was dead-tired and couldn't stop my mind from playing tricks on me. The bending trees made creaky noises. Dragging the sled through the frozen snow made loud noises. I was so scared that I started running on the slippery road. The sled turned over, spilling most of the yarn. Sweating and frozen at the same time, I finally reached the main road.

I crossed quickly, running the last two blocks. The whole family was waiting for me when I knocked on the front door. Wil was standing in the hallway. He hugged me. "We thought we'd never see you again," he said. It sounded like he had cried. Mother and Nettie hugged me, too. I couldn't believe it. They were worried about me. Wil looked at my hands and said, "Looks like frostbite. Let's put them in cold water to get your blood moving." I could not feel the icy cold water on my hands. When my hands started to tingle, he rubbed them. I looked at the clock on the wall. Three o'clock. I had been gone five hours.

"I want to take a quick look at what you brought home," Wil said. He emptied my pail in a large metal bucket, adding water and soap. I knew the soap wasn't even strong enough to clean greasy hands and I wondered how stinky the strands would be when Mother knitted with them. "Aren't they too short to use?" I asked hopefully. "Mother is a knitting genius. She can do it, "Wil answered. I knew then that I was stuck, having to make more trips. Mother made me a small meal and I ate slowly. They all waited until I was ready for bed. Bob had not made one nasty remark.

The next day, Wil washed the yarn, getting rid of some of the smell, but it was still very strong. The soap was made from clay, and it couldn't get the strong stink out of the yarn. They let it dry overnight, and Mother knitted a front panel for the first sweater to be bartered. The yarn was thick and heavy. I couldn't believe the speed she knitted the strands and how she guessed the number of stitches she could get out of a short piece of yarn. Since they were short, they had to be knotted on the inside of the sweater. The cut-off pieces looked to me like an itchy stubbled surface to wear. I was hoping she and Wil would think so, too. Wil said that it was great what I had done. Mother seemed to be happy with the way her knitting looked, and it felt good that Mother could make sweaters. I just hoped that the farmers would think them good enough to trade them for food.

The next day I told Wil the problems I had with the tools. "Let's go upstairs and see what we can do," he said. I was only allowed in the attic when I was with Wil, and then only when he was working on something that had to be fixed. The attic had a small workbench with a single light hanging over it. The rest was dark. It was cold, with a strong draft from two slits in opposite walls that had been covered with glass, but now were open to the outside. The glass had broken long ago. Rows of large trunks were along the walls. I asked Wil, "What's in the trunks?"

"Parts of these were filled with the grains and beans we had stored. The others are filled with Fred's junk."

"What kind on junk?"

"Nobody knows. He won't let anyone near them. I only know that they are unliftable. They're much too heavy for the attic. I don't know if you've noticed the big crack that's in your bedroom wall, but that happened after we started overloading the attic. There has been too much weight up here for a long time. Lately the crack has gotten much wider. It goes all the way into the foundation, from top to bottom of the house," he said.

"Wow," I said. "Is it dangerous?"

"Don't know, and don't care." He sounded grumpy having to make the tools for me. He was swearing when he couldn't find the stuff he was looking for. He knew I needed a longer tool to get further into the compartments, and he had to make it. After listening to him for a while, I got mad. "If you don't want to make the tools for me, that's fine. I just won't go any more. I am cold too, but it's much nicer up here than in the yard." He turned around looking very surprised. I expected a smack, but instead he said, "You're right, I'm a jerk. This is nothing compared to what you're doing. I'm sorry to be so nasty." That was all he said. He continued digging through the junk in the corner, finding a piece of pipe and a steel rod. He bent the end of the rod into a hook, sharpening it on the grinder. This was now long enough to get into the back of the compartments to get out the yarn. He made a handle from a piece of a broomstick, drilling a hole in the wood and pounding the rod into it. Covering it with rubber tape made the tool easier to hold. He cut a new pipe in half, telling me to slide it over the crowbar to make it longer. "You won't have to pull so hard," he said. While he was working, he talked to me. "How did you make out the first night?"

"I need protection for my face from the wind and snow." He knew the ski mask I wore was no good. "My breath kept freezing around my mouth," I told him. "Mother always uses Vaseline on her cracked fingers," Wil said. "That may protect your face from the wind." I had always wondered why she was putting that greasy stuff all over her hands and hoped it would keep my face from cracking.

"How difficult was it to get the compartments open? I've seen the springs on the covers. I know they're strong," he asked. "It's hard to crack the rubber seal. Pulling and turning at the same time takes all my strength," I told him. "I can imagine how difficult it is for a kid your size." He kept on asking questions. "The oil must be really lumpy," he said. "Yes, I got it out with my hand. It made my gloves sticky but warmed my hands. Why is that?" He smiled. "The oil is coating your hands. It works like an extra glove. It keeps the cold air off your skin. The more oil on your hands the better," he said.

Then he asked how afraid I'd been in the dark. "When I got to the road into the yard I was nervous. It felt like animals were hiding in the park. It was very scary." He hugged me but didn't say a word. He just nodded. Knowing that he knew my difficulties, and fears, made me feel a little better. "I don't want to open brake boxes that I have already emptied," I told him. "How will I know?"

"You can smear a handful of oil on a place underneath the floor of the car. This way you can check if this was one you already worked on," he explained.

I was surprised how nice Mother was when I returned from the trip. I hoped that she would stop protecting Bob, but that didn't happen.

With the trip to the rail yard, I had no time to visit Jan as much as I usually did. The following day I was so tired that I had to stay inside. It didn't take long for Jan to start asking me why I stopped biking. I felt terrible having to lie, but I told him I had been feeling sick. "I'm not surprised you're getting sick," he said. "We're all getting run down with having to eat the crap they feed us at the food kitchens."

SECOND TRIP

I had school for two days, paying no attention to the teacher. She was a nice lady. It was easy to be in her class, but I didn't listen to anything she said. I was tired and hungry. The next trip to the yard was all I thought of.

The days we had no school I stayed inside, telling Mother that I was feeling sick. "Stay inside and rest," she told me.

The days passed, and Saturday arrived. It was a clear day. Wil told me to get ready for my second trip. Enough snow had fallen to let me use the sled. In the evening he strapped two buckets on the sled, and I was on my way. "I can't come with you anymore," he said. "Being outside is too dangerous for me."

I walked in the shadows until I reached the main road. Crossing over took much longer because it was lit by moonlight. I had to wait until I saw no traffic coming toward me. Finally, it was safe to cross to the other side. I was worried about walking in the middle of the road into the yard. Anyone driving on this road could see me from far away.

The sidewalk had many trees. Metal posts were also in my way. I had trouble getting past them with the sled. In the moonlight I could see the entrance to the yard when I was halfway up the road. When I reached the entrance to the yard, I could see the closest parked rail-car. Some of the snow had melted, and bare areas were easy for me to travel through. The first car had no snow piles against the wheels. I quickly tested my crowbar with the pipe that Wil had made. The cover moved easily. When I stuck my hand in the opening, I knew right away what was wrong. Only a small amount of yarn. This one I had already opened before. I took a handful of thick oil, smearing it on the bottom of the car floor. The next one was harder to open. This seal had been closed for a long time. I got a nice amount of yarn out of this one. Three more cars filled my first bucket. I started to feel a little better. *If it goes like this, I'll be done soon*, I hoped. That was a mistake. I stepped in a large heap of snow. Falling, it turned my sled over, spilling my yarn. My leg felt wet. When I pulled up my pants, I saw a deep cut on the side of my leg. It was bleeding, hurting badly. I had a rag in my pocket that I used for blowing my nose. Tying it around my leg slowed the bleeding enough to finish filling the second basket.

Limping, I struggled through the yard, trying to avoid the piles of metal buried under the snow. When I reached the road, I could see cars passing by at the main road. The moonlight made the road look like daylight. I didn't want to use the sidewalk with all the trees and metal posts. I stayed on the middle of the road. I was in pain and very tired. *If I get caught, I'm in trouble anyway*, I thought. The bricks in the road were very slippery. I knew if I rushed, I would crash.

With my treasure I finally got to the main road. It was quiet and I limped quickly across. This time only Mother and Wil were waiting for me. They were very pleased when they saw the two buckets of yarn. I managed to hide my wound from Mother. Iodine on my cut was not what I was looking for. The next day, Wil washed the yarn, and Mother finished the first sweater in two days. It looked nice on the outside, but the cut-off knotted pieces on the inside looked terrible to me. "I wouldn't wear that, even in the freezing weather. It stinks and would itch like crazy," I said to Wil. "That's not for you to worry about. You get the stuff and we'll take care of the rest," he said with a smile.

Wil and Mother decided that one more trip was needed to get enough yarn for two sweaters. She needed two more buckets to finish number two. "That will be enough to find out if the farmers will give us food for them," Wil said. We waited for a snowy night. I was surprised that it didn't feel like I had another mountain to climb. The main road was empty. I reached the yard fast.

The first railcar was easy. The following two gave me trouble. I now expected some of them to be difficult and moved to the next one in line. Even though I had problems, it went fast. Soon I was on my way back home. Luck was on my side. I didn't fall, getting out of the yard quickly. I got to the big road fast and was home in no time. Mother knitted number two. Both sweaters looked great. They were thick and heavy. They would keep anyone warm in the coldest weather. I tried one on. The smell, with the knobby things on the inside.--I knew I wouldn't wear them even in the coldest weather. "I don't think anybody will want these stinky things, even though they look nice," I told Wil. *They better not look inside,* I thought. The itching on my bare neck was enough to make me wonder how they could trade one of those for food. "We'll find out soon enough," Wil said.

They decided to make a run to find out if the farmers would be interested in the sweaters. My three brothers would go in the late evening on a day when it wasn't snowing. Riding their bikes in the dark, with deep snow on the road, would be too dangerous. They waited for the right weather, then they decided to give it a try. We waited for many hours for their return. When they finally showed up, they had their side-bags loaded with vegetables, potatoes, butter, and eggs. The next day Mother made a great dinner. I ate so much, I thought I was going to burst. It was the first delicious meal we had in a long time. Wil was right. The sweaters were good to have.

LESS FEAR

I made many more trips into the yard. I learned where the junk was buried and knew how to get around it. I was always nervous, but it did not wipe me out anymore. Before each trip I covered my face with a thick layer of Vaseline, looking very shiny and greasy. Bob called me "the grease ball." I ignored him.

At the end of 1943, the Germans were stopping anyone outside, even in the early evening. I had to go later. I never had them close by, but I did have to hide a few times when I saw patrols far away. One was at the end of the yard, but they never came in my direction. If they had dogs with them I would have been in big trouble. To my surprise I had found a few compartments that had colored yarn mixed in. Mother saved the yarn from those. When she had enough, she knitted two sweaters with beautiful fronts. "I think we'll get more food for those," Wil said. He was right. They got double the amount of eggs and butter for those. Mother had shown Nettie how to knit the simpler parts. Together they could finish a complete sweater in a day.

Before every trip, my brothers planned the best way to get to the farms. They left on their bicycles late at night, keeping us worrying until they got back. Sometimes they asked me where they should go, since I knew the back roads so well and knew where the German troops were camped. The farmers knew that they would arrive late in the evening. They didn't care if they showed up on their properties. Wil said they probably had warned each other that my brothers could show up late at night.

I made about twenty trips, and two were enough yarn for one complete sweater. We all knew that my brothers would soon have to stop going out at night. Patrols were increasing and people were being shot at. One night when they came back, Wil's bicycle had a bullet hole through its frame. When Mother finished the final sweater, my brothers took their last trip. I knew I would miss the eggs and sweet-tasting butter.

RABBITS AND CHICKENS

One farmer gave Wil a present on his final stop at the farm: four baby rabbits and six little chicks. When he came back, late that night from the trip, he woke me up to show what he brought home. He said, "You'll have to feed them and keep their cages clean." I loved animals and these were cuddly and cute, and I didn't mind at all. Wil promised that we would put cages together. Next morning, we worked in the shed to build a home for my pets.

When Mother sent my brothers to the farms, she told them to get as many potatoes and eggs as possible. "Vegetables go bad, but potatoes and eggs can be kept a long time," she said. We stored them in the crawlspace under the house, which was cool. The potatoes sprouted but lasted until the winter of 1944. It helped our family survive the famine that started in the country in 1943 and that would get much worse during the winter of 1944. The winter of 1944–1945 would be known as the "hunger winter." Many people would starve to death.

A weed called "stinging nettle" grew in our area. It causes painful itching when touched. I was smart enough to stay away from those plants during my bike trips. I had been cutting grass in the park's field to feed the rabbits, but I could be seen from the road, which made be nervous. A big sign on the gate read, "STAY OUT." I was telling Wil how it bothered me to be in the wide-open field when Bob chimed in. He was in the living room listening to me talking about feeding the rabbits. He suddenly said, "I know how to feed the rabbits and it won't be hard to get their food." I was ready to tell him to shut up, but Wil stopped me. "Well, how would you do it?" he asked Bob. "Easy," Bob said. "Feed them stinging nettles. They love them and it's the best food for rabbits." I thought that he was up to one of his nasty tricks, but Wil seemed to believe him. *I hope you're wrong*, I thought. Bob went in the front room, digging a large book out of his mountain. He found where it showed the nettles, giving it to Wil. Bob was right. It said that nettles were rabbits' favorite food and listed it also as good food for people to eat. We had big problems getting even the smallest amount of vegetables, and eating nettles could help. Wil said that we should try eating a little to see if it tasted terrible or would give us cramps. The book said that people should only eat the leaves.

Wil told me that I should pick one full bag to try it out. We still had jute bags left over from the coal deliveries. Wil washed one, letting it dry in the sun. "If you fill that up, we can try it." We had an inner tube from a truck tire in the attic, and Wil made rubber sleeves to protect my arms while I cut the plants. He also told me to wear two pairs of gloves. "Don't take them off until you're finished cutting and have it bagged. Cut the stalks into small pieces. It will make it easier to handle this nasty stuff," he said. I was glad that this job could be done during the day. "Make a pile on the ground and when you have a fair amount, lay the open bag next to the nettles and fill it," Wil had told me. After a few trips I got the hang of it, making it easier than cutting grass.

The first time I came home with the nettles, I wondered what the rabbits would do. When they ate the grass, they always left a lot. I had wondered how they would like their new food. They almost ripped the nettles out of my hands. They ate half the bag. After I fed the rabbits, Wil told Mother what we were having as a vegetable for dinner that evening. I could see on her face that she thought he was crazy. He convinced her to let us try it. "You do the whole thing," she said to Wil. Cooking the leaves removed the stinging. We had a whole pot full, which shrank to a small amount when it was cooked. I was surprised. Wil, Bob, and I ate it all.

No matter how we praised it, Mother said she would never try it. The rest of the family also thought that we were crazy. They said so. I learned to cut large amounts of the nettles quickly, getting enough for the rabbits and us. Finally, Mother tried them. To my surprise, she said that they tasted pretty good.

MARY

On some days at the field, I'd seen a woman carrying a bucket. She was busy digging in the frozen ground when I was getting my rabbit food. It was time for me to find out what she was doing. She was not friendly when I got close and tried to hide what was in her bucket, but I saw right away that it was filled with potatoes. "This field was planted with potatoes until 1942. Some are still in the ground. If you're patient, and not afraid to do some hard work, you can find a full bucket in a few hours. Make sure you don't let anybody else know about this. There are just about enough for both of us," she told me.

Now, every time when I went out for rabbit food, I spent a few hours getting a bucket full of potatoes. The woman told me that her name was Mary. I told her my name: Eddie. As we continued to see each other in the field, she asked me how we made out with food at home. By now, we had used up most of the farmer's food. When I told her that Mother had started to give us smaller portions, she nodded. "I'm not surprised," she said.

I told her about the soup kitchen trips and the sugar beets. "We're still hungry," I told her. "Well, why don't you pick dandelions? They're a great vegetable. They're growing everywhere. My family was Italian, and we ate them all the time, even before the war. You can mix them with the sugar beets and the potatoes to make a good meal," Mary said.

I told Mother and she said we would try the dandelions. We were hungry enough to try anything. I made an extra trip to the field, getting a bucket full of dandelions. When Mother cooked them, we quickly decided they were pretty good. A little bitter, but a lot better than nothing. Feeding the chickens was another problem, but Bob solved that one too. "Chickens love worms. When you're digging in the field you should see plenty of them. Just bring a jar." By now we had also found out that the farmer had told Wil the truth. We shouldn't expect our chickens to lay eggs. All six were roosters.

The Germans had started conducting raids in our town. Males, from sixteen years up, were arrested and shipped to Germany to work in their factories. All I saw on my bike trips were women and children. At school, we had a female teacher for a short while. Then that stopped again. Going to school in the morning and returning home in an hour was now mostly the case. Other than Bob telling me I would be stupid forever, I was happy.

THE EELS

I biked as much as I could, mostly alone because Red had things to do for his mother. When I biked along a river, I noticed a man pulling things out of the water. He was on the opposite side, waving to me every time he saw me. After a couple of weeks, my curiosity made me bike across the bridge that crossed the river. I met him on the other side. He was an old man who seemed to be in pain when he pulled things out of the water. I asked him what he was doing. "I'm fishing for eels," he said. He showed me two buckets, full of live eels. I couldn't understand how he could catch so many eels without having a fishing pole. He said, "I don't live far away. If you come to my house, I'll explain everything."

"I can't, but I can come back next week," I told him. The next week, the old man was busy again in the same spot on the other side of the river. I biked around and saw that he had two full buckets of eels again. He told me that he lived in a small house and I could come with him. The only way to reach it was walking down a winding path in the middle of a dense, treed area.

While walking to his house, he carried the two buckets and I pushed my bike. He said, "You can leave your bike outside; nobody ever shows up here." For a moment I was worried about going into his house, but my confidence made me go in. *I can push him over and run away,* I told myself. Inside the house he had a fire going. It was warm. "Sit on the couch and relax," he said. He asked if I was comfortable. "I'm just waiting until you're ready to talk to me," I

said. "OK, when I'm done, I'll show you what I do with the eels."
When he came back in the living room, he looked clean with different clothes. He sat next to me. He seemed to be about the same age
as Jan. He told me his name was Mike. Then he wanted to know my
name. "Eddie," I said. "I like that name," Mike said. After a while he
got up. "Come with me," he said. In another room he had two bathtubs that were filled with water. He turned on a big light that was
hanging over the tubs and said, "Go look and see what's in here."
When I looked over the edge, I couldn't believe my eyes. Both tubs
were filled with life, wiggling eels. I tried to count how many there
were in each bathtub, but it was impossible. "Why do you have two
tubs?" I asked. "I'll tell you later," he said. Back in the living room
he told me how he caught the eels. "I'll get a dead animal from one
of the farms and sink it in the river with bricks. "

"Is that what you were doing when I saw you?" I asked. "Yes,
eels are scavengers that live in the carcass, eating the inside. I leave
it on the bottom for a week. When I pull it out, it's crawling with fat
eels. I add salt to the water in the tub and that makes them spit out
everything in their stomachs. After a week, I put them in the other
tub that's filled with fresh water. It keeps them alive until I trade
them with the farmers for food."

I had been at his house for two hours and got worried about
being late for dinner. "It's a long trip home, I should go," I told him.
"OK. When you come back next week, I'll make you a nice fried eel
sandwich." When I asked him where he got bread for sandwiches,
he laughed. "Eels are like gold. Everybody wants them. It's easy to
get bread when I have eels to trade."

The next week, on Wednesday morning, I couldn't wait to visit
Mike. I raced around to meet him. He was already packed up. When
we walked to his house, I could see that he was in pain. He put the
eels in the tub, washed up, and changed his clothes. "I'm tired. I
must rest before I make your sandwich," he told me. "Sit next to me
on the couch so we can talk a little." When I asked him if he was in

pain, he said, "Yes, my legs hurt from standing in the cold weather. The trip home with the buckets doesn't help either." I felt sorry for him and said, "Can I do anything to make you feel better?"

"Yes, you can gently rub my legs; that will help a lot." I didn't know how to do it. He took my hand, putting it above his knees. "Move them slowly up and down. Don't be rough, that will hurt me." After a while he said, "Can you now sit on the other side doing it the same way?"

"Yes, it's easy."

"That helps a lot," he said. I was happy that I could help him with his pain. After a while he got up and went into the kitchen. He took a fat eel out of the clean tub and cleaned it quickly. He fried it, giving me most delicious sandwich I ever had. When I finished eating, I felt as full as when my brothers had come back with food after their first sweater trip to the farmers. When I was ready to leave, Mike said to me that I should not tell anybody that I had helped him with his leg pains. "This must be our secret. You have to be quiet about it." I promised him that I would tell no one, getting ready to leave. "Does your family like eels?" he asked.

"Yes," I said. He took five big eels, cleaned them, and put them in a paper bag. "If they ask why I gave them to you, you can tell them that I had too many."

When I got home and showed them to Mother, she was very happy. "We'll eat them tonight," she said. I did not tell her that I wasn't hungry after the big sandwich at Mike's. In the past, when I had tried to tell Wil that I had done illegal and dangerous things, he had always told me, "War time means that we all have to try survive and I don't want to hear what you do during the day."

I kept quiet about Mike.

When we sat down for dinner, everybody—even Fred—was praising the way the eels looked on a plate. Wil had fried them, and everybody got a good chunk of the fish. It was delicious. Halfway through the meal, Bob, who was sitting next to me, tried to steal my eel. He had done something like this before, but I was usually hungry enough to eat fast, and there had not been much left on my plate. This time, I was still filled with Mike's sandwich and had left a piece of eel on my plate that I wanted to eat later. When Bob tried to swipe my eel, I stabbed him in the arm with my fork. He let out a loud scream. Wil saw what Bob was trying to do, and when Mother was ready to yell at me, he told her what was going on. Bob was sent upstairs, crying as usual.

Later I heard Wil talk to Mother in the kitchen. What he said made me happy. "Eddie is the only one in the house who has a chance to get food for us. Bob is a lazy kid who doesn't do a damn thing but sit on his ass all day. I think you should be nicer to Eddie and tell Bob to lay off with the pestering. We would all be in big trouble if Eddie had the same weak spine as Bob."

WORRIES ABOUT MIKE

That night, lying in bed, I thought of what had happened at Mike's house. I didn't want to feel guilty about promising Mike that I wouldn't tell anybody about helping to get rid of his pain, but I was thinking there was something wrong with the way Mike had acted when I was rubbing his legs. If I had not felt safe being in his house, I would probably have told Wil, but I didn't think it was dangerous for me to be with Mike. It felt nice to be with him, and I already looked forward to next week's delicious sandwich.

My weekly trips to Mike's house were the same every Wednesday. I now helped him bring the eels home by carrying one of the buckets. Afterwards, he made me something nice to eat. He was able to get eggs and milk from the farmers. Milk was something I had not tasted since the war started. When I asked him why it was so wonderful, he said it came straight from the cow. While we sat on the couch, I helped him get rid of pain in his legs.

I was still visiting Jan across the street as much as I could and thought that I should bring him an eel to see if they liked it. I asked Mike for an extra one. He gave me a big, fat one. *This one is for Jan,* I thought. When I got back home I ran across the street to drop it off. When he saw the eel, he called Magda over to ask if she could use it. "Are you kidding? You know that this is our favorite fish. I'll make it for tonight's dinner," she said. I was happy to see that they liked it. It had been a good day.

Every Wednesday thereafter, I dropped off an eel at Jan's. They were very pleased, but Jan started to ask how I was able to get them. I knew I could trust Jan, but I didn't tell him. He kept on asking, but I would not give him any information about Mike. Jan kept on saying, "Nobody in this world keeps on doing things without getting something back for it. You must tell me what's going on. I'm worried about what you are doing. It may not be safe." I said I was fine and went home. Thinking about what Jan had said made me wonder if I should continue seeing Mike. I could always tell the family that the guy who gave me the eels had moved. There would be nothing to explain. I liked Mike a lot, but I began to realize that it would be better if I didn't visit him anymore. I didn't know why, but I started to feel that it was not right for me to keep doing this. The next Wednesday, I decided, would be the last time. I had been visiting him for about two months.

When I got to the usual place, he wasn't there. I wondered if something had happened to him. First, I thought I should bike to his house to check on him, but I didn't want to go to his place alone. *I'll check on him next week*, I thought, biking home. The family was surprised that I came home empty-handed. When I told them that the fisherman was not there anymore, they believed me.

I was really worried about Mike. That I couldn't talk about it with anyone bothered me a lot. The next week was the same, no Mike. I went home, telling Jan what happened. "Look, I'm glad. I know that you were doing something that was no good. This is the best way to stop it. You don't have to tell me what you did, just don't go back anymore." All week I thought about going back to see Mike. I really liked him. I missed my visits, but thinking about what Jan had said made me accept to stop it. No more eels and no more Mike.

Red's mother had been sick. He told me that he would have less time to hang out with me. "I have to take care of her," he said. For the next few weeks I saw little of Red. He was busy with his mother. Each day he had to be home to let the doctor into the house. I understood that he had to do all this for his mom. I told him that I really didn't like him, so this was fine with me. We laughed it off. I knew that soon we would hang out again.

School was still on and off. I had plenty of time to do whatever I wanted. When I came back from my bike trip in the afternoon, I did the usual, going across to tell Jan what I had seen on my trips. I was excited, because I went to a different area where I saw many trucks and soldiers. I was sure he would be interested. I was disappointed to find that the store was locked. There were some women standing in the street who bought his water. When I asked them why he was not home, they said, "A Nazi car came today, taking him and his wife." I was worried about him and told Wil what had happened. "Don't get involved. The Germans must have had a reason to pick him up. Stay away and don't ask questions." Even though Wil told me to stay away, I checked each day to see if the store was unlocked, but they never came back. The store stayed closed for the rest of the war. I knew I had lost another friend. Jan's place was a second home for me, where I was always welcome, and I had really started to like Mike. Now they were both gone. I felt very alone.

ANOTHER MISERABLE JOB

The coal my father stocked before the war was long gone. We used the gas cooking top in the kitchen to take the chill out of the living room, but it was still very uncomfortable. "There's one way to keep our stove working, but for that we need coke. You'll have to get it, but don't worry; it won't be as hard as getting the yarn," Wil told me. That's how it started, but it wasn't long before I knew that it would be just as bad, or worse. The difference was that I would be covered in coal ash, instead of smelly oil.

I didn't know what coke was. Wil told me that coke came from the electric plant on the other side of the dike. "It should be buried in ash heaps on their grounds. Their generators are driven by steam turbines, and steam is made in boilers that are heated by coal. It's the same way as the water in Jan's store was heated, except it's heated to a much higher temperature. These boilers burn anthracite, which is a special coal." He made sure I understood. "The coal in those boilers doesn't burn completely. Partially burned coal is called coke, and it gets mixed in with the ashes. Our stove is made to burn coal, but I know it will work with coke. The coke is what you must try to get for us." He stopped explaining, and I wondered if he did it to see if I would cry. I didn't. He started again explaining how to get the stuff. "I don't expect the ash dump to be guarded, but there's one problem you'll have. It's a cinder that is formed when some of the coal reaches a temperature that is close to melting. When this happens, it becomes a large clump, called a cinder. The boiler operators pull the cinders out with rakes and they also get mixed in with the ashes. Those pieces are larger than the pieces of coke and have different shapes than the coke. You can feel that it's a cinder, but you'll have to do it with your bare hands. Your knitted gloves would just get ripped on the sharp edges. They wouldn't last long." *Yeah*, I thought, *I may not last long myself, having to do this in an unknown dark area with my bare hands.*

I knew the power plant was behind the high dike in the rail yard. I'd seen the smokestacks when I was in the park but never had the courage to climb the dike. With the speeding trains flying by on top of the dike, it was too scary. The lights on the locomotive had lit up the yard when I was getting the yarn, and I was worried enough to be seen in the yard. Now I would have to climb over this dike with my sled and bucket to get coke. Trains came from both directions, sometimes passing each other where I had to cross over the dike. I would have to get to the other side fast. Also, it was hard to hear them coming. They had surprised me when I was getting the yarn. I saw the locomotive lights well before I could hear the sound.

I was now eight years old and not many things scared me. I had done enough risky things. How hard could this be? Couldn't be harder than going to the train yard in a howling snowstorm. It didn't take long for my optimism to change to big worries.

"Mother and I feel very bad about having to send you out on another dangerous trip again. She was against having you do this. I told her that it's the only way," Wil said. He held me by the shoulders, speaking softly. "We can't keep on heating the downstairs with the cooking top. It's too small. And running it all day is too expensive. The gas bill is already enormous, and we're bundled up and still freezing. Something must be done. Having you collect the coke is the only way," Wil said.

The next Saturday night, I was on my way to the yard again. I didn't want to reach the tracks using the approach road. I had told Wil about my problems getting the sled through a hole in the fence during my yarn collection. "You're now strong enough to lift the sled over the fence. Use the park to get to the tracks. That's best." I waited on the side of the main road until it was safe to cross and lifted the sled over the fence. I threw the bucket and tools over the fence and crawled through the fence hole. I quickly got to the far side of the park. The fence on this yard's side had holes large enough to put the sled through. With snow covering the ground, the troubles started as soon as I began crossing the tracks. I knew there were four sets of rails, which I remembered from the yarn trips, but I hadn't realized that this side of the yard had rail switches. The switches were used by the operators to steer the cars to different tracks. I could barely see the switches in the dark. Everything had to be done by touch. Climbing over the thirty-foot snow-covered dike got me nervous. I worried about the trains. The steep side of the dike made it very hard. I slid down part of the way a couple of times before I reached the top. Getting down on the other side was easy. I put the shovel in the bucket, letting my sled slide down on its own. I sat down on my rear, going the same way, just getting wet from the snow. The electric plant had an area that was used for storage of large construction materials. It was hard to cross with my sled and buckets. I also had to pass a block of houses next to the plant before I could reach the place where I thought the ashes would be. It was pitch black. I could only see shadows in the distance. I kept on going farther into the place, finally seeing a large pile in front of me. I wasn't sure what it was until I dug into it, feeling a piece of coke, buried in a large amount of powdery ash. "It's called fly ash," Wil had said. Even a little wind blew it all over the place, including my face. In the dark I could hardly see what I was doing, digging with my bare hands. As Wil had said, it would be hard to not cut my fingers on the cinders.

It was cold, snowing lightly, and it took longer than I expected, but I filled one bucket with coke. Climbing up the side of the dike was more difficult than before. I kept on sliding down, almost losing my coke supply. When I reached the top, I was anxious to cross before a speeding train arrived. I kept on hesitating, taking a long time before I made it to the other side with my bucket. Then I had to go back, climbing up again with the sled behind me. It was tiring me out fast. I couldn't let the full bucket go down by itself. The sled went down on its own, but the bucket was hard to control. One step at a time, digging my feet into the snow, finally got me down. It was hard to find the hole in the fence in the dark. *I must mark this spot for the next time*, I thought. The trip home was quick through the park. Shoving the full bucket through the hole was hard, but I managed. I threw the sled over the fence and crawled through the hole. I saw no cars coming and ran home.

I slowly started to relax a little after being home. Wil decided to see how the coke would burn. He put a few pieces in the heater. They were hard to start, but when they burned, they gave off a lot of heat, burning much slower than coal. The pieces lasted a long time. The next day I woke up late and thought I wouldn't get breakfast, but to my surprise, Mother had it all set up for me. She even asked if I had recovered from the trip. It was unbelievable. Wil said he was happy that I had been able to do the job. "Was it harder than getting the yarn?" he asked. "Yes, it's very hard to see where I was going. Tomorrow during the day I want to look."

SURVEILLANCE

I went again through the park. Now that it wasn't dark, I could pick the easiest place to cross the four sets of rails. I knew that I would need some sort of marker to make sure I could find my crossing place in the pitch-black. The switches were in front of me, and I decided where I should cross. There was a narrow path between the park fence and the first set of rails. I could easily follow that from where I crawled through the hole to find my marker. A ditch on the side was filled with branches and leaves. I found a metal pipe and a stick in the gully. With a rock I pounded the stick in the ground close to the hole in the fence and the pipe in the ground in front of my crossing spot. That would be the place where I had to get to the dike. Here, I would have only one switch to avoid.

These switches have a large lever with a heavy weight to keep them in position. I had bumped into one on my first trip, which gave me a painful bruise. At my crossing spot I could see that going straight across was the best way to avoid them.

I climbed up the dike to look on the other side. Standing on top gave me a clear view of what was in my way. The ash heap was about 200 feet from where I planned to get over the dike. Large boxes were stored on one side. Those seemed to be all I had to pass. Knowing how slippery it had been to climb the dike with the sled and tools, I reminded myself to use the small shovel. That way I could dig out steps to get to the top.

The following Saturday evening, I was on my way again. Quickly reaching the yard and following the fence, I found my pipe. Crossing the sets of rails and feeling my way around to see where the switch handle was, I stepped in the movable area of the switch. This was a space about four inches wide. My shoe sunk all the way to the bottom. The moving part of these switches is tapered and sharp, and I got a cut on the side of my foot. I tried to pull my foot out, but my shoe was stuck, and I was only able to pull it halfway up. Then it got caught on something that I could not see in the dark. No matter how I tried, it would not budge. After panicking, I knew that the only way to get my foot out was to untie my shoe. It was hard to reach the double-knotted laces. It took a long time. It was easier to move the shoe around without my foot in it, and I finally freed it. I had been standing in the snow, without a shoe, and my foot was nearly frozen. The snow had stopped the bleeding. Now it was just hurting. Pain was something I was used to, so it was not enough to make me turn around empty-handed. I was gonna get my two buckets of coke, no matter what.

It took time to get the shoe back on my foot. My hands were cold, and it was hard to tie the laces. Now the dike. I dug small steps in the snow with my shovel, slowly reaching the top with the first bucket. My foot was hurting badly. I had to go down again to get the other bucket and sled. I brought a penny with me, which I put on the rail. I waited for a train to speed by. I knew kids on my block who had done the same thing, and I'd seen what happened to the penny. They were flattened, very thin, becoming three times as large when the train's wheels went over them. If it worked, that would be my lucky penny. I hoped it would. I needed some luck. When the train passed, the penny was where I'd put it, thin and large. Climbing down on the other side, I made small holes with the shovel to put my feet in. It worked. I didn't have to slide down, getting my pants wet from the snow. I could see the boxes in the distance. When I passed them, I saw the pile of ash in the distance.

Remembering how the blowing ash had burned my eyes, I walked around the heap until the wind started to push me forward. That was the best side for digging. I dug with the shovel until I felt it hit something. It was a large cinder. I used my hand to check for coke, finding a fair amount of coke close to where the slag was buried. I would have to ask Wil why that was so. It could not just be luck. With the shovel I dug out the cinders, which spared me from many cuts on my hand, and I was able to fill two buckets in a short time. The return trip was also faster. Using the steps I had dug made it easy to cross the dike.

I collected coke for a few weeks, knowing what to expect. One Saturday evening I set out at the usual seven o'clock, getting to the storage area at about eight o'clock. Something had changed. My usual ash heap was gone. I stumbled around in the area, finally finding one in a different place. I lost a lot of time and had little luck getting my usual amount of two buckets. Somehow, these ashes were different than the old ones. They were warm, which was strange. I lost track of time and kept digging, but I found little coke. It was almost as if this pile had burned more completely. The coke pieces that I found were smaller than what I was used to, and there were fewer cinders. It was taking much longer than usual to fill my buckets. I didn't want to go home empty-handed and kept on digging. When I didn't return after my usual three-hour trip, the family got worried. Finally, Wil set out to find me. It was very dangerous for him to be out at night. From my description of the place, he knew where to cross over the tracks into the power plant area. He finally found me, half frozen, but still digging. He took me, and my stuff, home. He started the heater with the coke to warm me up. "We don't want you to freeze to death. The coke is not worth losing you. You agree, Mother?" I looked in her direction and she nodded.

The following week I found the "strange" heap, and another one next to it. I stuck my shovel in the ash of the one I was used to and found coke with fewer of the usual pieces of cinder. I kept

on digging, quickly filling my two buckets. Wil said, "They probably switched boilers to have one to work on. The one they fired
up produced a different type ash. Once at full temperature they
were back to what you're used to." I took these trips weekly until
the end of the war without major problems. I got some injuries
along the way but was able to keep the family from freezing with
my fuel supply.

INTO HIDING

The Nazis were conducting raids, slowly reaching our suburb. The only place my brothers could hide was in our crawl space under the house. It was a few feet high and clammy, smelly, and drafty. Wil showed me where they would have to stay, and it made me as nervous as I'd been on my first yarn trip. "We'll need sand to build a berm to protect us from hand grenades the Germans drop down the trap door in the halls of the houses they're checking," he said. "We'll have to protect ourselves against the blast."

Bob and I got the sand from a block away where a tree had blown over, using a cart that Wil had made. The job had to be done in the dark, which made Bob afraid. He insisted that we overload the cart, and a wheel collapsed. Wil had to come out of hiding to replace the wheel. Bob blamed me, and Mother believed him. "Bob is too smart to have done that," she said. "Don't tell me that," Wil told her. "Bob is lazy and didn't even want to help. It's time that you stop blaming Eddie and admit that he is the only one who can get us to survive this damn war." The three occupants of the crawl space living quarters dug out a space far from the trap door opening and fitted it with planks from the attic and mattresses. Wil called it "the nest." Raids were getting closer, and I kept an eye on them.

THE SOLDIER

We expected raids to be in our area any day now. One morning, loud talking from the neighbors woke me. Usually I didn't pay much attention to street noises, but this time I felt that something was wrong. A raid was happening on the next block. It would soon reach us. Mother was already out of bed. She had started the heater, making it warm in the living room. When I got downstairs she said, "Get Nettie out of bed, and tell her to fix her hair. She has to look good." I didn't understand but did as I was told. A little later Nettie came down, looking nice with her enormous amount of curly hair. We waited nervously, and finally a loud knock on the front door warned us that somebody dangerous was outside, ready to check the house. Mother said to Nettie, "You go let them in and don't forget to smile."

I was sitting in front of the heater with Peeps, the cat, on my lap, when the door opened. In walked one soldier with a rifle over his shoulder, a pistol at his side, and a long overcoat. This was the first time I had ever seen a real soldier in front of me, instead of sitting in a truck. He looked a little older than Bob. He let Nettie walk first into the living room. I expected the worst, but all he did was look around for a minute, taking off his long overcoat and putting put his rifle and pistol on the table. I had heard some of them were bad and I was afraid he would kill all of us, but he was nice. When he sat down, Mother told Nettie to sit next to him. Mother saw that he was more interested in her than anything else. He kept on staring at Nettie, and she didn't know what to do. He smiled a lot and she squirmed. Then he noticed me with the cat on my lap. He held out his arms to show me that he wanted to hold the cat. When I handed Peeps to him, I thought he would be clawed. This cat was not friendly with anyone, but he snuggled right up, settling on his lap. It was hard to believe. Mother spoke a few German words, and with hand signals we found out that his name was Heinrich. He was from the town of Wiesbaden. He had a mother and sister in Germany. He went into the army at the age of seventeen. Mother made him a cup of tea. He stayed about a half hour and left. It looked like he wanted to stay longer with us, but he had to go. Instead of looking at the house, he had looked at Nettie. Nettie had not known what to do when the soldier stared at her so much. Nobody had ever done that. When he left, he kissed Mother and Nettie on the cheek, which I thought was very nice of him.

Nettie immediately went upstairs after the soldier was gone. She would not come down to help Mother with preparing dinner. I was told to get her. She was lying in bed, red-eyed, telling me she felt sick. I asked her why she had been crying. She got mad, yelling at me to get out of the room. Everybody had been shaken from the close call. That Nettie seemed to be upset was easy to see and that she was acting strange didn't bother anybody. When I asked her if it was because of the soldier, she got mad and screamed to mind my own business. Mother had always kept her away from boys. She was told to stay away from the boys her age, who lived on the next block. They had asked me a few times why we were hiding that nice-looking sister. A few days went by and she was fine again. Then she said a crazy thing to me. "I want you to start looking for Heinrich," she said. "He was very nice to us. I want you to find him, so we can thank him." Each day, when I came back from my ride she would corner me, asking if I had any luck finding him. My answer was always "No such luck."

We all realized how fortunate we had been during the raid. If he had checked the house, he would have seen my brother's bicycles in the shed with a bullet hole in Wil's bike. I had heard that some of these soldiers would shoot their guns through the floor and would listen for moaning when someone was hit. We had been very lucky.

RISKY BEHAVIOR

Regular radio news programs in Holland had stopped during the first years of the war, and all that was heard on the radio was German propaganda. We listened to the English BBC news program at night, but that was very dangerous. It was done by Wil sticking a needle in a cable that ran under the gutter in the back of our house. He would poke around with the needle until he found the right wire in the cable. It was a terrible connection with loud static, but it was all we had to hear Allied news. We heard that the German troops were still fighting fierce battles in Holland, and it looked like the war would not end soon. Mother finally told Fred to make us a better radio, and he build a contraption on a piece of plywood. I thought it would catch fire, but we heard the depressing BBC news from England without much static.

Patrols had increased and I had to cut my coke trips to one per week. We used the gas heater and wore more layers of clothing. One day I came back from biking and found Wil in the hallway working on the gas meter. "Now we'll have free gas," he said. "Turn on all the burners," he said to Mother when he was done. He had bypassed the gas meter with a piece of inner tube from a bicycle. When it was time for the meter reader to show up he would remove the tube. It worked great for a while until the guy showed up unexpectedly. It took Wil ten minutes to hook up the meter. The man was banging on the door with Mother on the inside shouting, "I'll be right there."

"We have a gas leak and I have told the company many times," she told him, when he asked where the gas smell came from. From then on Wil only bypassed the meter after dinner for a few hours.

The raids in our neighborhood had moved to other areas, and Wil told me to find out where they were. I didn't see any German activity anymore, and I told him it looked safe. "We want to start sleeping in the bedrooms again. You'll have to make sure that there are no surprise raids going on." I checked and people told me that raids never took place at night. "There are still a few Dutch soldiers around who would like to kill some Germans in the dark," they told me. That allowed my brothers to stay out of the nest.

Dutch families living in the neighborhood, who were cozy with the Germans, openly partied with them. They informed the Nazis on anyone they suspected of hiding Jews. They also turned in men who were hiding. I knew which people to stay away from. Wil told me that they would be taken care of after the war.

Conditions in the country were now miserable for almost everybody. Food and fuel were impossible to find. Many people were starving and freezing. The 1944-45 winter was very bad. It was hard to get potatoes and dandelions. We survived on the few potatoes I could still dig up and dandelions. That, mixed with sugar beets that Mother had saved was all we had.

It was now very risky to go on my single weekly coke trip. With our little gas heater, some coke, and the field pickings we survived the terrible winter.

MEAT AGAIN

Our rabbits were fully grown and ended up on the dinner table. The meat was incredible, and Mother made great soup with the bones. The roosters were next. Wil had skinned the rabbits in the toolshed, but the roosters had to be killed on the patio. Bob had to help me. Wil told him to hold the bird by the legs and head and I would chop his head off. Bob was scared to death. Wil warned him not to let the bird go, but Bob hadn't listened. I chopped off the head, and he let the headless bird go. It took off, hitting him in the chest. He screamed and ran in the house, covered in blood. Mother must have thought I had tried to kill Bob. We had six roosters, and each time we had a circus on our patio. I was sure the neighbors thought we were a bunch of crazy people.

It was now March 1945, and hunger was everywhere in the country. My small pickings from the field were not enough to keep us from starving. Wil had been eying Peeps, our cat. This cat was big, and we were hungry. The cat lost. Wil did the dirty deed. Mother made delicious meals and soup from Peeps, who rescued the family for the second time. I still remembered how the cat had distracted the soldier.

The Allies were bombing German cities each day, and planes were passing over our town every night. German troops were shooting at the planes, but they were high in the sky. Wil said that they would be lucky to hit a plane. Well, one night, luck was on their side.

The normal engine droning sounds suddenly changed to a loud roar coming from a plane, passing low over our house. A few minutes later the house shook from a big explosion. "The pilot had to drop his bomb load to prevent crashing on the houses," Wil said. We went back to bed, but I had trouble sleeping. I expected another plane to hit our house. The next morning I biked to where I thought the bomb had hit. The place was roped off, but that didn't bother me. The bomb had exploded in a canal that was between two rows of houses. This canal was always filled with muddy, stinky water, but it was now almost empty. Most of the mud was piled on both sides of the roads, sticking to the walls of the houses. Live fish wiggled in the mud. I quickly found three big fish and took them home. We all spit them out after the first bite. Tasted like mud.

Every night we listened to the BBC newscasts on the radio, and it was reported that the German army was close to being defeated. Rumors were that the war was over, and people started dancing in the streets. Wil and I went outside to take a look. When we turned the corner, three German soldiers were shooting at anyone who was outside celebrating. After a few more weeks it was finally over. It was May 1945, and we could go safely outside.

FOOD DROPS

Food deliveries started, and our town was next. They dropped big boxes from airplanes on the park and potato fields where I picked the nettles. I saw the boxes swinging under big parachutes. It was a windy day, and some parachutes drifted away from the drop area, hitting the streets, many splitting open. Delicious white bread and chocolate were all over the roads. Good times had finally arrived. After that, they quickly switched to truck deliveries. Food distributions were set up in the park and the potato field. The park's handouts were done by Americans. Bob, Nettie, and I went as many times as possible to load up with goodies. For two weeks they didn't question anyone, but then it changed. Once a week was now the rule, and they remembered who the cheaters were. After that, Nettie was the only one who got extra portions. With her great looks, the soldiers liked her more than Bob and me. Mother questioned why she did better than Bob and me, but Wil told Mother to quit picking on her. "You should tell Bob to do a better job and be happy with what Nettie is doing it for the family," he told her. I was surprised that she didn't yell at Wil.

The Canadians were very hard to fool. They always remembered who we were, and many times they sent us home empty-handed when we showed up more than once a week. Even Nettie had little luck. One day, when they told me to get lost, I checked the area where they set up their tents. On the field I discovered a pit they had dug for their kitchen garbage. Garbage was not all. It also contained utensils, pots, pans, and furniture. I also found "live ammunition". I stuffed my pockets full and showed them to Red. We opened one cartridge and found yellow strings inside. We lit a few, and they burned with an intense bright yellow flame. We had to handle this stuff carefully. We rolled a bunch of strands in newspaper and taped it. With bricks supporting it, we launched our rockets. The flame was very strong, and we worried about it landing in a back-yard, starting a fire. I took another trip to collect more cartridges, and we set off a bunch of rockets in the nearby canal. We quickly got bored and quit.

A neighborhood kid's father was a chemist. He showed us the description for making an explosive mixture from sulfur and salt-peter from one of his father's books. Red and I could easily buy those chemicals from a local pharmacy. They were cheap. Why not give it a try? It could be fun. The store sold us a pound of each. Our friend had warned us that it had to be mixed carefully. "If you put too much pressure on the mixture during mixing, it will explode." I took a small spoon of each, mixing it on the sidewalk in front of the house. We decided to test a little of the mixture by hitting it with a hammer. It exploded with a loud noise and a good size flame, but it seemed safe. It was not as powerful as the cartridge strands. I'd seen a box of large bolts in our attic that were left over from my father's collection days. I remembered two of the bolts were large, each with a nut. We put the powder in the thread of the nut and carefully screwed the nut back on the bolt. If we threw the bolt on the side-walk, the nut's friction would set it off. It worked well, producing a loud bang. The bolt jumped up about a foot. We decided it was safe. Of course, even though it worked fine, we had to try different methods. Red started mixing little heaps of the powder on the side-walk, hitting it with the head of the bolt. It made a loud noise, with a nice flame. For a while, he seemed to be satisfied with that, but not for long. He started to increase the amount of mixture. "You are taking a big chance with your hand so close," I said to him. "Don't worry, I'll be careful," he answered. He hit a large pile with the back of the head of the bolt and gave out a loud scream. The flame had cut right through his middle finger, leaving a bleeding stump. I didn't see him for the rest of the week. When I saw him, his hand was heavily bandaged. "I can't use my hand for writing. The teacher told me to use my left hand," he complained to me. "It's very hard to write that way."

I should have used that method so that they could not have forced me to write with my right hand, I thought. *What could the straight edge teacher have done about that?*

Red would not touch the mixture anymore. Without him it wasn't much fun. He threw the rest of his portion in the sewer. I decided to hold onto it a little longer. I stored my bags in the rabbit cage in the backyard. When the bandage came off Red's hand, he was without half of his middle finger; just a short stump left.

For many weeks we didn't discuss my leftover portion. I didn't want to take a chance with the bolt anymore and was thinking about dumping my stuff too. Then I thought of putting small portions on the track of the high-speed trains. The sound would just be like a bunch of firecrackers going off. Small amounts would not be dangerous for the train. "Let's go to the yard. We can put some of our powder on the tracks," I told Red. I had a pre-mixed bag of the powder in my pocket. We used the approach road, walking far into the yard while staying between the row of rail cars and the dike. We were just about ready to climb up the dike when two people appeared with a dog, at the far side of the terrain. Red saw them and yelled, "Patrol!" We crawled under the cars, taking off toward the fence. The fence was higher than my head, but I managed to pull myself up, to swing over to the other side. The bag of powder in my pocket got caught on top, and my weight caused the mixture to ignite. A flame shot out of the front of my pants while I fell on the ground on the other side. Red was already over the fence. He saw it all happening. He told me later that I gave the loudest scream he had ever heard when I took off across the field. "You broke an Olympic record running home," he said. Mother nearly fainted when I walked in the house with the front of my pants blown off. We went to the doctor who took care of Dad. "What happened to you?" he asked. I decided to tell him the truth. He cut my pants open, cleaning the burn. It was terribly painful. He smeared some lotion on, which only helped a little. He gave the rest to Mother. When we left he said, "You're extremely lucky that the flame went outward. If the flame had gone inward, you would not be here." The next day I dumped the rest of the powder in the sewer.

REVENGE

Two months after the war ended, people in our town went after the rotten traitors. They were rounded up and driven through the streets on flatbed carts. This period was known as "Ax Day." Everyone was on the street, waiting for them to pass. There was lots yelling and swearing from people standing on the sidewalks at those we hated so much. The women had their heads shaved and swastikas were painted on their heads with hot tar. Many on the sidewalks threw rocks at them. Adults standing on the curb hit them hard. Every time someone hit them in the head there was a lot of applause. They were also throwing paper bags full of shit at them. Some of them were covered in it. *That's what they deserve, those bastards*, I thought. Their houses were emptied, staying locked for a long time. Nobody wanted to live in those places.

After four months, conditions returned slowly back to normal. School started again, and I was stuck five days a week in a stuffy room, hating it. The teacher was the nicest we ever had, but I had a hard time sitting in the classroom all day.

Fred and Wil volunteered for a three-month time to clean up German ammunitions, left when the German Army was defeated. They both were assigned to clear storage areas, used by the Germans outside our town.

I was slowly getting used to a more normal day, doing a few loops on my bike around the block and then to school. Brother Nick had left to live with his girlfriend. I was glad he was gone.

Weekends were the best for me. I looked forward to Wil being home on Saturdays. He showed up with a smile, had a beer, and leaned back in the chair with his feet on the table. He told Mother and me what happened during the week when he was cleaning up the explosives around the countryside. He always made it a funny story. I hung on every word, listening to him.

SCOUT AWARD

It was Saturday afternoon when the doorbell rang. Mother said, "Go check and see who it is." When I opened the front door, I almost fell over. It was Magda, Jan's wife. She smiled at me, asking if Mother was home. I said, "Yes, she's inside."

"Go tell her that I need to talk to her for a minute, please," Magda said. Mother never wanted to talk to strangers. She refused until I told Wil who was at the door. "It's OK, Mother. It's the wife of the man who sold us the hot water for all these years. Go see what she wants," Wil said. Mother went into the hallway, talking with Magda for a long time. When she came back into the living room, she said that Magda would be over to visit the following Saturday and that the whole family had to be there to meet her. On Saturday, Magda rang the doorbell at five o'clock in the afternoon. Wil knew her very well. He welcomed her into our house. We were all wondering what she had to say. Mother had made a pot of tea, and after Magda was settled in and introduced to the family, she started to talk. "You may know that my husband Jan and I were arrested by the Nazis. We were taken to the jail in Utrecht. When we got there, we were separated, and I never saw Jan again. The guards told me that the following morning he was shot with two other men who had also been picked up the same day. I was told that an informant had turned us in. 'Don't deny what you've been doing. We have proof,' they kept telling me. Magda continued explaining that she was interrogated daily. This lasted six months. She claimed that Jan had never told her anything about what his activities were. They finally decided to let her go.

Now that the war was over, she thought that it was time to tell my family what role Jan had played during the war. In the same sentence she also mentioned my name, as if I had been part of this. When she was talking and mentioned my name, everyone's jaw dropped, including mine. What was she talking about? Then she began. "Jan was one of the leaders in the resistance movement in our town. Their job was to make the occupation by the Germans as difficult as possible with sabotage, which they did at night. Their difficulty was always getting information about troop sizes, number of vehicles, tanks and locations. This is where Eddie came into play," Magda said. "When Eddie showed up with his bicycle, telling Jan he liked numbers and knew how to count, Jan figured that this could be a way to have Eddie give him numbers of trucks driving by. Jan was very worried about having him do this. He was only five years old, but he decided that it was the only way to get the information." Now the rest of the family understood why Magda had visited us. She was here to tell the family what I had done. There was more to come.

"To thank Eddie for what he did, and to remember Jan, the surviving members of the movement are having a small event to celebrate the end of the war. I am here to invite both Eddie and Wil to the meeting, next Saturday afternoon." She left, after saying goodbye to the family. I told Wil that I didn't want to go. "Nonsense," he said." We never knew that you were so important in all this." Wil and I went to the meeting the next Saturday. The room was filled with people. I tried to sit in the back, but it didn't work. Wil and I sat with Magda in the front row. They had a cake and Magda talked to the group. I was too nervous to listen. They gave me box and I had to open it. A picture frame was in it. It read:

To Eddie Schrama.

From a grateful people for exceptional accomplishments during trying times.

The Dutch flag was painted on it, with a picture of Jan and a group of people I had never seen in my life. On the bottom were many signatures.

Wil was poking me in the side, telling me to stand up, but I was too nervous. Finally, I managed to get up. I turned to Magda and said, "I am very sad that Jan died. He was like a father to me." There was a lot of applause when I sat down. I was very glad it was over.

They had a big cake with my name on it. Everybody got a slice, but they left my name on a big piece. Magda said, "take it home and show it to the family. They will like that very much." Nobody was interested when we got home and I was not surprised.

"They're jerks; don't worry about them," Wil said.

THE EXPLOSIVES

After the war there were parties in the street with loud music. Wil and Fred were still clearing out the ammunition storage places. Fred had found a plastic-type explosive that was stored in a steel case. It was labeled TNT. The boxes weighed twenty-five pounds each and could be taken home on his bike's luggage rack. Over time, he brought home ten cases, including hundreds of detonators, which were quickly brought up to the attic by him. Nobody cared about what he was doing. Food supplies were slowly coming back in the country, but fresh fish was still not available in the stores. Before the war, my brothers had fished in the canal where Red and I shot our missiles into the water. At that time they had caught some nice fish, but now they weren't in the mood to use fishing poles. Instead, they used the explosives. When dropped in the water, the explosion would kill fish close by but stun others, far enough away. All would float to the surface and they would scoop up the live ones. We had no boat, and they pulled the fish in with a long rake, standing on the water's edge. Wil had taped broom handles together to make the rake long enough. They had a clean jute bag with them and filled it with fish, loaded it on their bikes, and returned home. They did this a few times, but decided it was too risky and stopped. I didn't mind. I was sick of fish already.

Mother had little interest in what my brothers did. What got her attention was when a bad storm came through our area. Warnings on the radio about dangerous lightning conditions were predicted, and we had a house full of explosives that could blow up the neighborhood. Fred and Wil came home in a panic and told everyone, "Take a case of explosives and stand in the doorway, with the case between your legs."

"What is wrong with you?" yelled Mother, but Fred ignored her. Mother stood, with everybody else in doorways, balancing a steel suitcase filled with bomb material between her knees. That's when I saw Mother flip out, which had not happened in a long time. "You are out of your mind to have brought this stuff home. What were you planning to do with it?" she screamed at Fred. He had no answer for Mother and just stood there. She made it very clear to my army brothers that the stuff had to go, and that night they took a couple of bicycle trips dumping the TNT in the canal. Fred still had the collection of detonators and flares. He assured Mother that those were safe. "Nothing to worry about," he said.

Flares were used by the German Army to signal battle conditions. These were fired into the air with a special pistol, which we didn't have. Wil made a firing mechanism with two planks that were hinged and a hole to stick in the cartridge. A nail was used as the firing pin. They set them off in our tiny backyard, with our neighbors on top of us. Fred had a large collection of different colors. He set them off and they went high up just like they were supposed to. They exploded, way up in the sky, with beautiful colors. On wash day, laundry was hung outside on lines all around us in the back yards. Fred set off a dark blue cartridge, which misfired. It barely got higher than our house, landing with a graceful arc in the middle of the neighbor's laundry a few houses over, where it exploded. All the laundry in their yard was dark blue. The neighbor came out screaming and swearing, but Fred thought it was funny. When Mother found out, she told him to get rid of that "crazy stuff you two brought home." That night the canal was visited again. Now, all that was left were the detonators.

Fireworks were not available after the war, and people were still celebrating, so Wil used Fred's detonators in the street. We had three different kinds with delay fuses of five, ten, and fifteen seconds. These detonators had an aluminum tube with a powerful charge inside. Wil set them off by holding a wooden match against the open end of the fuse. The fuse would start to burn, making a sputtering sound. He always used the fifteen-second delay. The shorter-timed fuses did not give enough time to safely get away from the blast. One night, Wil and I went out to set off some bangs in the area. No problem, until he dropped one off very close to a Salvation Army band that was playing on a corner. They scattered in all directions. Wil said that one guy almost swallowed his trumpet. He acted like he thought it was funny, but I knew their reaction had shaken him up. Scaring people like this was not what he wanted to do. The next night started the same way as before. Wil set off the detonator, throwing it in the middle of the street. A little boy standing on the sidewalk saw this sputtering thing lying on the ground and started running toward it. Wil ran across the street dragging the kid away. He was about fifteen feet away when it went off. We went straight home. "We're done with these," he said. That evening, the detonators also went into the canal. With luck and living dangerously, we had survived five terrible years. Many others didn't. It had been a harsh set of events that shaped my future. Wil and Fred took jobs in other towns and would only be home on weekends. On one Sunday afternoon, Wil told me to walk him to the bus stop. "I know you're unhappy that I'm away all week, but you have to accept that I can't stay here forever. You had much harder things to deal with in the last five years, and you handled those better than many adults could have done. I've never told you how much I admired how you coped with the terrible conditions I put you in. I can't think of anyone who could've done for the family what did. I know for sure that any difficulties that come up in your future will be easily handled by you." He hugged me and stepped on the bus.

I walked to the park entrance and sat on the grass, thinking how it would be without having Wil around. The three months when they were doing the work for the army hadn't been too hard. Now it felt like he would be gone forever.